The Lit...

WOMEN'S
WISDOM

The Little Book of
WOMEN'S
WISDOM

Judy Ashberg

PIATKUS

For Leah, a very special person

Copyright © 2001 Judy Ashberg

First published in 2001 by
Judy Piatkus (Publishers) Ltd
5 Windmill Street
London W1T 2JA
e-mail: info@piatkus.co.uk

**For the latest news and information on all our
titles, visit our website at www.piatkus.co.uk**

A catalogue record for this book is available from the British Library

ISBN 0 7499 2247 8

Design by Paul Saunders

This book has been printed on paper manufactured with respect for
the environment using wood from managed sustainable resources

Typeset by Action Publishing Technology Ltd, Gloucester
Printed and bound in Great Britain by
Bemrose Security Printing, Derby

Contents

Understanding Yourself

It is very difficult to live a happy life if
you don't actually like yourself.

The first person you must learn to love
is yourself. When you are able to love
yourself, all other kinds of loving
become easier.

You can have as much love in your life as you want. It is all there waiting for you. Start loving yourself and more love will definitely follow.

Beauty alone does not make a woman sexy. If you feel good about yourself, you are sexy.

It is okay to want to feel sexy
and attractive. Why else would we have
been created this way?

Some women are too hard
on themselves, judging their own
actions more harshly than they would
ever think of judging anyone else's.
You do not deserve to receive such
unkindness and criticism from
anyone, let alone your
own self.

Many women aspire to do everything perfectly. When you can accept that this is not possible, you will become more relaxed and receptive to other things and the people around you.

Although there are always
people who are worse off than
you, sometimes it is helpful to
acknowledge that you are the one
who is having the bad time.

Some women live their lives
behind a mask, carefully weighing
up everything they say and do in case it
is 'the wrong thing'. Likewise, many
women have been brought up to be
'good girls', to be 'seen and not heard'.
When we reach adulthood we need to
recognise that we are as good as
everyone else and we must speak
up for ourselves.

We are all wise women.
If we take the time to stop being
so busy and to quieten our minds and
reflect, we can access that part of our
consciousness which can help us
find the answers to
our problems.

We are all special and have
our own unique spirit and presence
which is unlike that of
anyone else.

Always try to have an interest
or a creative outlet for yourself.
Every woman needs to tend to the
essence of who she is and develop her
special talent. If you do not know
what yours is, either you have
not yet found it, or you have not
acknowledged it.

Some women feel guilty if
they are not working all the time.
Give yourself permission to stop and
do something for yourself –
or simply just to stop and be.

We need to be attuned to
our own needs, wants and desires or
we will be unable to live our lives
to the full.

We do not have to wait for other people to give us permission to try to be anything we want to be. The first step is recognising that we can give this permission to ourselves.

Sometimes, whatever you do
for the people you love, it isn't
good enough for them. Sometimes this
is because nothing you will *ever* do for
them is adequate because they do
not feel good enough about themselves.
What you can acknowledge, both to
them and to yourself, is that what
you have done is good enough for you.

If we can do things for others
we will feel happier in ourselves.
But beware of doing things for
others all the time and
neglecting yourself.

Some women think that unless
they fulfil other people's needs all the
time, no one will love them. When their
own needs go untended, those
women are often the
most unhappy.

Some women care too much about
what other people think. They let
others have too much power over the
way they live.

You do not need to worry what
other people think of you because most
people are much too interested in what
is going on in their own lives to be
interested in yours.

People who put you down and belittle you on a regular basis are not the right people to spend your time with. If they choose not to change, you must ask yourself why you are choosing to share your life with them.

If something in this book arouses
unexpectedly strong feelings in you, for
whatever reason, it is a clear indication
that you need to think carefully
about this particular aspect of
your life.

Beautiful women and those
who have shapely figures do not
necessarily enjoy happier relationships
or better lovemaking than
you do.

Look after your body in the
same way you look after your most
cherished possessions. Care for it and
treat it well. It is the only one you
have and it will need to last
you a lifetime.

Many of us worry far too
much about what we look like. We
need to remember that what is really
important is who we are and how we
live our lives.

If you find it hard to think of
yourself lovingly, try this simple
exercise. Once a day look at your face
in a mirror and say out loud, 'I love
you'. With practice you will find this
easy to do and you will be
surprised at how quickly you
start to love yourself more.

Parents
and Children

Every child wants their mother
to love them just the way they are. If
your mother cannot do this, try sending
her love from your heart. Even though
you may find her difficult to
communicate with, sending her
love can often generate love
in return.

When you are an adult and
you hear your mother's voice in your
head telling you what to think and what
to do, you need to stop and ask yourself
whether those instructions are still
appropriate for you and the life you
are living now.

The relationship with your mother
can be the most wonderful, loving
and nurturing one in your whole life. Or
it can be the most difficult. Sometimes
there is not a lot that you can do to
change the relationship, but try to
learn from her mistakes and achieve
something better with your
own family.

It is very easy to blame our
parents for things that have gone
wrong in our lives. Why not spend time
acknowledging all the positive gifts they
may have given you which have
enabled you to achieve
something better?

The greatest gift you can
give your children is to love
them unconditionally.

When you have children who
love you and whom you can be proud
of, you are truly blessed.

Many mothers find their
daughters difficult to relate to and
understand. Many of the conflicts
between you may be caused because
you are both so similar. What
we may hate or despise in ourselves,
or what we may yearn for, becomes
much harder to bear when we
see it in our daughters.

Some mothers need to learn
that their daughters are not an
extension of themselves. They are
separate individuals with their own
thoughts, minds and beliefs.

When our children are growing up, we need to take extra care of ourselves, both physically and emotionally. It is a heavy burden for a child to live with a mother who is often ill or unhappy.

We cannot make up for
being working mothers by buying our
children clothes and toys. But we can
learn to listen to them so that they
feel 'heard' by us. This is one of
the greatest gifts we can
give them.

Learn to listen well to your
children and acknowledge what
they tell you. If you can be with them
and respect their differences, without
judgement and without criticism, you
will have a wonderful relationship.

Children will always respect
you if you apologise to them when you
are in the wrong.

Children are much happier when
parents set clear rules and guidelines
and stick to them. But there are also
times when parents need to be flexible.
Knowing when to stand firm and
when to give way is one of the
great skills of parenthood.

If you are not living with your children's father (and also if you are), however strong your feelings and however hard it is, try not to speak badly of him in front of your children. They will have a much greater chance of happiness in later life if they are able to have a good relationship with both parents.

If we constantly find fault with
ourselves and what we say and do,
we cannot be surprised if our children
grow up to have low self-esteem.

Some women expect their families to read their minds. This never has been and never will be possible. We must all learn to speak directly and say what we need to.

The things we think are
unimportant are often the things our
children will hold against us later in life.
The things we think will be important
to them often do not matter in
the slightest.

If parents and children can all
enjoy one meal a day in each other's
company, that is more important
than all the things that money
can buy.

Some parents are so enmeshed with their children that it can be difficult for these children to separate from their parents and find out who they really are. The major task of parenthood is to encourage eventual independence so that our children can take their place in society as happy, healthy adults with purpose in their lives.

There is no such thing as a perfect parent. All parents make mistakes in bringing up their children. We have to learn to forgive ourselves and acknowledge that parenting is the hardest work we will ever do. We cannot expect to get everything right but we must be satisfied that we are 'good enough'.

Not every woman is able to conceive, and not every woman is suited to being a parent.

Always treat your children equally, however hard it may be. Some children are easy to love; others are more difficult. The more difficult the child, the greater the challenge and the more joyful the reward.

Not everyone, parent or otherwise, will find our children as interesting as we do.

If you are living with children
who are not your own, try to love them
unconditionally, however hard it is.
Sometimes nothing you say or do will
make a difference but you will know
that you have done your best and
that is all you can do.

Women often live their lives
through their families and do not make
time to acknowledge their own needs
and abilities. When children leave home
and partners grow old, they may find it
difficult to create a life of their own as
they have had so little practice.
Pay attention to your
own needs.

However much we may strive
to love our children, we may still be
disappointed in them. Are our
expectations of them realistic?
Or are we simply seeking to
control them?

If you want a happy household
and you want your children to be good
friends when they are older, never
compare one child with another,
or play one off against
the other.

Some children are difficult and misbehave because we are not giving them enough attention. It is not enough to be with them physically; we have to be with them emotionally as well.

Sometimes our children grow
up and reject us and what we believe in.
This does not always mean that we were
bad parents or they were bad children.
Sometimes they come back; sometimes
they don't. The only thing we can
do is to keep loving them and
respect their decision to lead their
lives the way they want to.

Children who have grown up
without much love in their lives will
find it difficult to give and receive love
when they are older. We need to
recognise that these people require
extra compassion, love and care,
especially from those who have
always been loved.

A good, loving mother,
grandmother or mother-in-law never
behaves like a martyr.

Be kind and respectful to
your son's partner and try not to
criticise or judge her, however hard this
may be. When she is on your side,
life is so much easier.

The perfect grandmother is a paragon of virtue. She is loving and helpful, never interferes and never offers an opinion unless invited to do so. We can but try!

Not many people are
experiencing the family of yesteryear –
mother, father and two children living
together happily ever after. Our real
'families' often consist of all the
people who we love and who
care about us, whether they
are related or not.

Relationships

New friends are silver, old friends are gold. This saying isn't always true but when it is, we are very blessed.

Some friends are always there
during the good times; others rush to
help at the bad times. True friends
rejoice at your good news and cry with
you when you are sad.

Some women have friends who
need a lot of support; other women
need a lot of supporting. Find friends
who can be there for you when
you need them as well as
when they need you.

Sometimes the people we find
the most difficult to deal with in our
lives are the ones from whom we learn
life's greatest lessons.

Betrayal by a women friend often
hurts much more than betrayal
by a man.

Do you always support your friends in times of trouble, but find that when you need a friend, no one is there for you? Ask yourself what you are doing to attract all these needy people into your life. Some people are so needy and self-absorbed that they sap all your energy. You can still love them but you may decide to limit the time you spend with them.

Be kind to men for they are as vulnerable as you are. They are simply better at hiding it!

Women are often attracted,
whether consciously or unconsciously,
to men who are like their fathers. Be
aware of this, and study the men
you fall in love with
very closely.

Restraint is always a virtue in
relationships. Always show tact and
respect at the same time as
being honest.

All successful relationships
contain elements of compromise. We
have to recognise that we cannot always
have what we want – and how little
some of the things we think we
want really matter.

When we care about the people
we live with, we often do their
emotional work for them. Your
anger, envy and jealousy may not belong
to you; it may be your partner's
unacknowledged feelings that you are
experiencing and acting upon.
Learn to know the difference
between what is his and what
is yours.

Sometimes the people we love
do not love us back in the same way.
They do not want or need the love we
are offering them. This is one of life's
most painful lessons.

The old saying that the way
a man treats his mother is the way he
will treat you is always worth bearing
in mind.

Everyone experiences at least
one difficult relationship in
their lives.

Men respond positively to
happy women who
like themselves.

Men want to spend time with a
woman who knows her own mind, is
kind, loving and a good listener
– and has a sense of humour.

Take your time in choosing the
person you want to spend the rest of
your life with. This is the most
important decision you will
ever make.

The more love you give to the man in your life, the more you will get back. Stay true to yourself and do not change to please him.

The cause of most relationship breakdown is poor communication. People do not communicate well either because they don't know how or because they have fallen into the habit of not communicating. Once we recognise the problem there are many ways to improve communication skills and transform the relationship.

Many women do not realise how
constant criticism can destroy a
relationship until it is too late.
Respect your partner's differences and
do not try to change him. Surely you
would not want him to treat you
any differently?

Sometimes we expect the men in
our lives to be perfect; sometimes the
women. We have to remember that we
ourselves are not perfect – and nor
is anyone else.

How wonderful that men and
women were created to relate to one
another in the way that they do. Living
happily ever after with the right partner
is about achieving intimacy, love,
contentment and harmony of
the highest order.

It is rare to find a man who can satisfy all our needs. Much better to recognise that, as well as a partner, we need several people in our lives, all of whom have something different to offer.

Equality in the home does
not mean being unkind to one another.
Always treat your partner with the same
respect that you want him to
show to you.

Many relationships continue
for years in pain and misery because the
woman chooses not to find a way of
expressing what she wants
and needs.

Accept that some men are not good at acknowledging emotional occasions or choosing the perfect present. It is much better to remind him of the date and ask for what you want than to sulk or get angry because he doesn't have the skills to fulfil your romantic fantasies.

Many women become bored with the men in their lives and think they could find better elsewhere. Take a good look at your relationship before you decide to move on because another woman may bring out in your man all the qualities that once made you fall in love with him. And remember, it is always possible to fall in love with the same man twice.

If you have never experienced at first-hand a good relationship between a man and a woman, it can be difficult to know how to achieve it for yourself. Try to spend time with happy couples of any age and observe the dynamics of their relationships.

The qualities that attract us in a man, before we set up home with him, will often be the same qualities that we argue over so painfully later on.

Sometimes we can live with
people for years but never be truly
intimate. Intimacy requires trust and
commitment, openness and honesty. We
must never take advantage of our
partner's vulnerability, for intimacy
can only be experienced when
both partners feel safe.

When we engage in a sexual relationship where there is little or no commitment we may become very vulnerable, even though we might not admit it to ourselves. Think carefully about your sexual partners before you allow them into your life. Although we live in liberal times, not everyone is suited to having casual sex.

Being a good lover takes practice.
And even when you have made
wonderful love with the same person
many, many times, no two experiences
will ever be quite the same.

Personal
Growth

The most difficult work we can ever do is on ourselves, trying to understand why we are as we are and why we behave in the way we do. If you take the time to do this work, you may find that happiness and peace of mind are your reward.

We are so used to living our
lives in different roles – daughter,
mother, sister, wife – that we sometimes
forget to use our own voice. We
need to speak out and be true
to ourselves.

Some women enjoy the role of victim and martyr. It can be difficult to persuade these women to change because, if they do, they will have to grow up and take responsibility for their actions. It is easier for them to blame all their troubles on other people and events.

If you find yourself constantly
drawn to look after other people,
whether friends, family or co-workers,
you may need to recognise that this
could be a substitute for all the
times in your life when no one
was looking after you.

Wisdom and guidance are available
to us all the time. From professionals
and individuals to books, magazines and
specialist organisations, there is
always some way we can find
help for ourselves if we choose to
look for it.

The people who achieve the most success in life are those who are brave enough to take risks. This has nothing to do with your family and where you came from and everything to do with who you are now and how much courage, will-power and self-determination you possess.

We need to acknowledge that we all have a shadow side. Sometimes we project feelings we do not recognise we have on to other people; sometimes we cannot see that the characteristics we dislike so much in others are very similar to our own.

Sometimes we are angry with people
or dislike them because we have not
acknowledged how much we want
to be like them.

Do not be quick to judge others.
What we think we see on the surface
may be completely wrong. We never
know what is really going
on underneath.

As we go through life, we
change and develop. As we do so, we
must recognise that others are changing
too. We must be able to forgive the
past and move on to
something better.

A woman's life is defined by
the way she lives it.

If you had an unhappy childhood,
you can choose not to live as an
unhappy adult. But, in spite of our best
intentions, we sometimes need guidance
and support to understand how
our past has affected
our present.

Women are naturally tender,
caring and compassionate. We must
remember not to lose sight of these
qualities when we enter the
often harsh world of
the workplace.

You can change your values and beliefs once you have recognised what they are and where they come from. Sometimes the values we live by come from early childhood and we do not even realise how much they affect our lives. Sometimes they are opinions inherited from other people and no one has challenged us really to think about them.

When we are little we often
construct elaborate defences to cope
with emotions and situations which we
find painful. When we are older these
familiar defence patterns are often
still in place and we do not
realise that we no longer
need them.

There comes a time when every woman needs to recognise that she is no longer a child and has become an adult. Some women never manage to do this. These child-women are often very unhappy, not recognising why they find it so difficult to relate to other people.

Every woman should try to have some money of her own so that she can have some control over her life. Equally, every woman should learn how to manage money so that she does not find herself powerless and vulnerable. Managing your own money takes practice but is not difficult. Do not let anyone convince you that it is.

We must learn to speak up for ourselves so that we are paid the same as men for the same job.

When you make a decision to follow your heart, especially in difficult circumstances, the universe will recognise your courage and commitment. You will find that the expected obstacles fall away and the road ahead is clear.

There are many lonely people
in the world. Sometimes we need to
choose the right person to open up to in
order to share our pain. This act of
courage will help to mitigate
our aloneness.

Everyone is unique but you
can learn a lot from the people you
respect and admire.

We all worry too much. What are you afraid of? Ninety-nine per cent of the things we worry about never come to pass.

If you are not used to praying, it is easy to associate it with negative images from your childhood. But praying as an independent, mature adult can alleviate worry and anxiety.

Prayer is a private conversation.
You can say whatever you need to in
order to unburden yourself. Always
think carefully about what you
pray for because prayers are
often answered.

Happiness and
Inner Peace

Happy is the woman who enjoys
who she is and what she does all day.
The secret of a happy life is to
develop a happy mind.

❀

as the right to be
happy. We will never feel good about
ourselves if we cause unhappiness
in others.

Happiness is waking up in the
morning and looking forward to
the day.

Happiness is being able to love
and be loved. It sounds simple,
but one of the hardest challenges in
life is achieving successful
personal relationships.

Happy children laugh a lot. Adults laugh much less. The more opportunities you give yourself to laugh, the happier you can be.

If you were in another world and looked down at your life in this one, what could you do to make yourself happier? And what might you want to change?

We need to look after our own health so that we can enjoy life to the full. Never neglect yourself because you believe you are too busy.

If you are often ill with minor
complaints, you might want to
ask yourself why. Is this the only way
you can gain attention
for yourself?

We live in a consumer society
where many people earn their living
from persuading us to buy things we do
not need or want. Happiness comes
from within and not from what
we buy.

Happy is the woman who can control her hours in the workplace. This freedom to work at the times which are best for you is one of the most important things to fight for.

Happiness comes from being kind,
loving and compassionate. It is
hard to be any of those things if you feel
bitter and angry. It is always possible to
change the way you live your life
deep down and see things differently
but no one can do this work
for you.

If you are feeling sad or depressed,
ask yourself, 'What can I do now, at this
moment, for myself, to make me feel
better?' Then do it.

It is important that you follow your heart as much as you can throughout your life. If you do not, you will feel cheated by life when you are older and it is too late.

❀

can have too much love.

to give out more love than

we receive, we are truly blessed.

It is easy in our busy society to lose sight of what really matters – love, kindness, compassion, thoughtfulness, generosity, caring. If you can keep sight of what is really important, your daily troubles will seem insignificant.

We are constantly bombarded
with stories of brilliant women who do
wonderful things. We need to recognise
that not everyone is or wants to be
ambitious and career-driven. We need
to find a way of using our own talent
and creativity that is right for us, and
not try too hard to model ourselves
on some unattainable ideal.

Sometimes we are overwhelmed
by all the anger, grief, sadness and pain
in the world. We cannot always help as
many people as we want but we can
make an effort to get our own lives in
order and set a good example to
those around us.

Some of us are given more in life; others are given less. We must learn to share what we have. In our material society this can be difficult, but we need never feel guilty about the gifts we have been given if we are able to share.

Your mind is not separate from your body. If you are ill, you need to look more closely at what is going on for you emotionally. Your body is sending you a clear message that you need to stop what you are doing and rest. Try to take the time you need to get properly better and use the space to think carefully about what is really going on in your life.

It is only our bodies that need to grow old. Our minds can remain as youthful as we want them to.

Sometimes an aspect of our behaviour troubles us so much that we have no choice but to seek help. Acknowledging and overcoming our fears of vulnerability can often lead to much greater peace of mind.

If you know you are doing
everything you really want to in life at
the time when you are able to do it, you
will never look back with bitterness
and regret.

When you are old, you will not remember how clean and tidy your home was, but rather how much and how often you laughed and enjoyed yourself with those you love.

If you set aside time from your
busy existence to develop the spiritual
side of your nature, even in only a small
way, you will be moving towards
greater peace of mind.

Women are naturally spiritual
and intuitive. Paying attention to your
unexpected thoughts and feelings
can lead to better health
and wellbeing.

Make an effort to spend more
time in the fresh air; it will not only
improve your health but it will raise
your spirits.

When you suffer loss it can be hard to find comfort. The only thing we know for sure is that life is cyclical and winter will always give way to spring, even though sometimes it takes a long time to come.

We live in a very competitive society. Sometimes we do not realise how much time and energy we use up in competing with family, friends and relations to have something better or to be something better. We need to recognise how pointless much of this is and concentrate on enjoying all the good things we have already.

Some women live in the past;
others are always planning for the
future. If you want to enjoy life, the best
place to be is here, and now.

Some women are born with
great gifts: beauty, intelligence, wealth.
But the greatest gift of all is to live your
life loving others and being
surrounded by people who love you.